house beautiful

BEDROOMS

house beautiful

BEDROOMS

The Editors of House Beautiful Magazine

Louis Oliver Gropp, Editor in Chief ~ Margaret Kennedy, Editor

Text by Cara Greenberg

HEARST BOOKS
NEW YORK

It is the policy of William Morrow and Company, Inc., and its imprints and affiliates, recognizing the importance of preserving what has been written, to print the books we publish on acid-free paper, and we exert our best efforts to that end.

Library of Congress Cataloging-in-Publication Data

House beautiful bedrooms / the editors of House beautiful magazine:
    Louis Oliver Gropp, editor in chief; Margaret Kennedy, editor: text by Cara Greenberg. —
1st U.S. ed.
               p.   cm. — (Great style series)
      ISBN 0-688-12587-5
        1. Bedrooms.   2. Interior decoration.   I. Gropp, Louis Oliver.
    II. Kennedy, Margaret (Margaret S.)   III. Greenberg, Cara.
IV. House Beautiful. V. Series.
NK2117.B4H68   1996
747.7'7—dc20   95-38384
                                       CIP

Printed in Italy
First Edition
1 2 3 4 5 6 7 8 9 10

Edited by LAURIE ORSECK ⁓ Designed by NANCY STEINY DESIGN
Produced by SMALLWOOD & STEWART, INC., NEW YORK

Contents

Foreword

The one exception to the generally simple, modern things in the Gropp household is our bed. It belonged to my wife's uncle; her father shipped it across the country to us after his brother's death. The bed is big and curvy, and it has dominated the decoration of our bedroom throughout our long married life. I'm not sure that I like it as a design, but I know it has played a central role in my family's life. I never feel more at home than I do when I climb into that tall, comfortable, and oh-so-safe piece of furniture. And I have wonderful memories of our two daughters, when they were much younger, clambering in to join us there on lazy Saturday mornings.

Let's face it: Bedrooms are important. The most personal and private of all the rooms in a house, they shelter us and our guests, provide comfort when we are sick or tired, and give us a space in which to enjoy our dreams.

Over the years we have found that readers always respond positively to *House Beautiful* issues that show a bed or a bedroom on the cover. Perhaps it is because these are the rooms we often wait to "do" after the more public rooms in our house are "done." That may be a mistake. *House Beautiful Bedrooms* was designed and written to help you correct that mistake as soon as you possibly can.

Louis Oliver Gropp
EDITOR IN CHIEF

house beautiful
BEDROOMS

Introduction

To the long list of things we take for granted these days, let us add the bedroom. It wasn't very long ago that separate chambers for sleeping were unheard of, and privacy for the individual was a completely foreign notion. In medieval Europe, whole families slept in the same hall-like room used for cooking, eating, and even sheltering animals. In the seventeenth and eighteenth centuries, to escape the hubbub in the main hall, some clever, well-to-do individuals conceived the idea of separate rooms for sleeping. By the mid-nineteenth century, bedrooms were commonplace throughout the Western world.

Yet in our fast-paced society, private time and space still seem elusive. The bedroom is more important than ever as a retreat, not just from the more public parts of the house, but from the chaotic world outside. With this primary purpose in mind, the decoration of a bedroom becomes a challenge of the most pleasant sort. The exact forms this may take vary widely ~ from lavish to spare, from traditional to idiosyncratic.

House Beautiful Bedrooms offers abundant proof that decorating the bedroom can inspire great flights of imagination. The boundaries of what is "permissible" have become wider and more expansive than ever, as we draw our inspiration from diverse cultures and the entire history of design.

On the pages that follow, you will find much of what you need to know to create the bedroom of your dreams. But we also hope you will enjoy simply perusing these beautiful rooms, and that you will begin to see their design possibilities in a new, more brilliant light.

CHAPTER 1

Setting a Mood

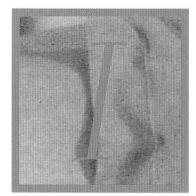 n the geography of a house, the bedroom is the most private sanctuary, a place blessedly free from the public eye. The very appeal of a bedroom is that it is one's own, a place to go and close the door on the world. It is only natural that it is our most personal expression, the most self-indulgent of rooms.

Many people would say a bedroom should be restful, in keeping with its primary function, or perhaps romantic ~ billowing curtains, soft rugs, subtle lighting. But not everyone feels that way. "The bedroom should be as exciting and stimulating as any other room," says one designer, who uses lively colors, bold furnishings, and busy fabrics to implement her vision. "Cheerful by day, sultry by night," says a woman who, confined to her bedroom for months during a difficult pregnancy, chose a metallic wallpaper that metamorphoses by the hour with the changing light.

Whether the ultimate effect is clarity and calm, or a more energetic state of being; whether the desired feeling is historic or of the moment, sophisticated or rustic ~ the bedroom can truly be the stuff of dreams.

SERENE RETREAT

Two hundred years ago, a bedroom was called a cabinet, and it was often just that: an alcove in the wall, with panel doors that could be pulled shut for privacy.

"That's exactly what I wanted ~ a real getaway," says Spruce Roden, a New York City floral designer, of the master bedroom in his Connecticut country house, a central-chimney colonial dating from 1788. The decor was inspired even more specifically by a suite of Federal-period rooms at the Brooklyn Museum in New York City; Roden loved their clean lines, spare furnishings, and palette limited to just two colors. He captured that serene mood by designing a gleaming, snug, wood-sheathed box that gives its inhabitants the illusion of being totally removed from the workaday world.

The house, though old, was not historically important. "It had been messed up so many times, it gave me a certain freedom to mess it up my own way," Roden jokes. But he did make an effort to be true to the Federal period by restoring architectural details that had been stripped away during several zealous renovations. In the master bedroom, the walls were clad in raised pine paneling custom-made in the style of the eighteenth century, then painted a luscious blue-green. New closets, lined in cedar, are hidden behind doors covered with matching panels, which unify the room's perimeter and complete the effect of an

The lush romantic painting above the bed ~ a landscape coincidentally dated 1788, the same year the house was built ~ serves as decorative headboard and also keynote for the color of the walls, a true-to-period blue-green. Creamy linen sheets add to the restfulness and tranquility of the room.

enclosed "cabinet." Many of the furnishings and fabrics are true to the period, including a cherry four-poster bed.

Roden's masterstroke, lending distinction and a certain dressiness to the space, is the coffered ceiling, crafted by a local shipbuilder. The original beams, ravaged by age, were encased in pine boards, then painted glossy white. The result is a comforting space, far removed from the demands of the twentieth century.

Wool damask, the fabric of choice in fine Federal homes, is used for the sofa, draperies, and bedspread. An acorn-and-oak-leaf pattern echoes the acorn motif found on the four-poster's finials. The gold-trimmed sofa, a 1920s copy of a piece found in England's Knole castle, sits in front of a small French Directoire table. Both face a fireplace ~ a luxury on winter nights. The brass wall sconces are modern copies of a period design.

A ROOM WITH TWO VIEWS

The drama inherent in this Manhattan bedroom comes from the dynamic interplay of opposing energies. Owners Katie Ridder, a designer with a fondness for the decorative objects of the Middle East, and her husband, architect Peter Pennoyer, like things crisp and clean ~ and rich and sultry at the same time. The bed's white sheets, and the snappy blue and white striped curtains, for example, could belong to a beach house, while the richly colored folding screen and the arabesque-patterned wallpaper are evocative of a Turkish bazaar.

It is in fact the wallpaper that ties the room's two "personalities" together, literally reversing itself and transforming the mood of the room as the hours go by. By day, the walls are bright and reflective, making the room a cheerful afternoon retreat. Come nightfall, by the glow of brass table lamps, the metallic sheen of the paper tones down to matte, and the atmosphere becomes muted, romantic, mysterious.

At night, especially, the room seems removed from the city that surrounds it. "I love bedrooms that take you away from your environment a little bit," Pennoyer says. "The boring thing is to do a bedroom in a modern apartment pure and white." It is more interesting, he points out, to strike a completely different mood from the rooms you encounter on your way there.

The room's approach to color ~ a subtle handling of the three primaries ~ is a daring one. The warmth of the gold wallpaper makes the space seem to glow as if from within. The blue adds a complementary note of coolness. And touches of red in the fabric screen add interest to an otherwise nondescript corner. Ridder had originally chosen a complex-patterned fabric for the curtains, but Pennoyer vetoed it as "too expected." The couple opted instead for the lighter feeling of the blue and white stripe. The overall effect is energetic, eccentric, and offbeat ~ in a thoroughly comfortable, even luxurious, way.

Color, pattern, and time periods are mixed with assurance in this big-city bedroom. An eighteenth-century straight-legged side table in red maple and a brass lamp by early modernist designer

Walter von Nessen share a cozy corner. The headboard and bedskirt sport the same summery blue and white fabric as the curtains. Simple sisal carpeting quietly pulls the room together.

A *screen made from fabric from a 1920s theater set incorporates the three primary colors that dominate the room's palette (near right). Amid the exuberant pairing of pattern and color in their master bedroom, white bed linens and a white-draped nighttable provide a few oases of calm (far right). A yellow slipcovered vanity chair keeps company with a birch Biedermeier-style dressing table, crafted in Scandinavia in the 1870s (below right).*

AUSTERE BEAUTY WITH A PAST

*I*t takes a reverence for the past to appreciate the gentle, evocative beauty of the rather spare guest bedroom in this 1762 clapboard relic of colonial New England. Here, the mood is one of deep repose. "We wanted to keep it tranquil and calm and authentically of the period," says one of the owners. "Nothing glitzy or jarring that would make someone say, 'Yes, they must have redone this place in the late eighties.'"

Carefully edited and composed by master designer John Saladino, the room is as dignified and pure, and as starkly dramatic, as a Quaker meetinghouse. Yet it also radiates great warmth. "I wanted it to glow at night like the inside of an old lantern," says Saladino. And so it does: The desired rich tallow color was achieved in a two-step process. First, solid ochre paint was applied to the walls as a ground. Then, in a paint technique known as sponge-glazing, a warm cognac color was layered over it.

In fact, the walls in the guest bedroom were the only surfaces that were painted. The original paneled door and window moldings were dry-scraped and intentionally left in rough condition. That approach coincided with the owners' treatment of the entire house, which had never been modernized. Over the generations, numerous coats of paint and wallpaper had virtually encrusted every room. Most surfaces were simply hand-stripped, then left alone, resulting in the mottled, corroded look of broken walls unearthed at an archaeological site.

A pair of reproduction Shaker-style cherry wood beds, their canopies undraped, are compatible with the pristine starkness of the space ~ a starkness relieved only by a pair of white heirloom candlewick coverlets crocheted by the grandmother of one of the owners.

The conscious restraint shown in furnishing the room is in deference to the house's age. Citing details such as the original wide panel doors, the elliptical arch of the fireplace, the wonderful patina of the window casing, and the old glass in the panes, Saladino says, "If we had overfurnished it, some of those subtleties would have been lost."

Even without a blaze, the pure lines of the guest bedroom's big working fireplace are a strong focal point in this New England landmark remodeled by John Saladino. Flanking the hearth are a Mission-style oak chair by Stickley Brothers and a genuine Shaker rocker bought at auction. The kilim rug brings out the cinnamon color of the walls.

There was no need
to fake age in this house.
An appreciation of
its effects is evident in
the treatment ~ or rather
nontreatment ~ of the
scratched and worn
bedroom door, moldings,
and trim (above left), as
well as the window
moldings left unrestored
and bare (below left).
Crocheted bed coverlets
paired with heavy
khaki and cream-striped
canvas spreads and
a geometric-pattern rug
provide softness in
an otherwise austere
room (opposite).

GILDED SIMPLICITY

Only a very skillful mood-maker like Charles Spada could take two very different qualities ~ guilelessness and sophistication ~ and play them against each other so as to bring out the best in each. "I love incongruous things together," says the Boston-based interior designer. This Connecticut stone house, built a century ago by a Tuscan immigrant and refurbished by Spada, retains all the unpretentious roughness of an old-world dwelling. Yet its furnishings, mostly European antiques of good pedigree, reveal the cultivated tastes of an esthete.

In the renovation of the second-story bedroom, as in the rest of the once-disastrous interiors, Spada encouraged the rustic nature of the house, built from local stone and hand-mixed sand mortar, to shine through. The designer deliberately left the floors bare, bypassed wallpaper and printed fabrics, and used only white paint on walls restuccoed in the crude European manner.

The bedroom's original low pine ceilings (only 6 feet 8 inches high) and wide-board wood floors form an envelope for outstanding antiques. The highly polished woods of the eighteenth-century pieces and a gilded Italian mirror are lustrous against the matte finish of the stucco walls. The overall effect is intentionally spare. "When a room is terribly filled with color and objects," says Spada, "you can't concentrate on anything."

Deep-set casement windows reveal the sturdy construction of this old New England house. Shown off against the original wood ceiling and old wood floors of the master bedroom, fine antiques ~ a gilded Italian mirror, Swedish grain-painted writing table, cane-back French chair, and English bench set at the foot of the bed ~ add notes of sophistication and polish.

Questions of Balance

he most successful decorating is often a delicate balancing act, a tightrope walk between playing it too safe and going over the top. A bedroom that is "all one thing" ~ religiously of a single style or period, say, or burdened with an overabundance of pattern, or spare without relief ~ can quickly become tiresome.

Dynamism comes from the conjunction of opposing elements, whether in terms of texture (the roughness of a sisal rug against the sheen of highly polished woods, for example), color (a jolt of bright red against a pale background), or attitude (a seashell on a fine antique piece).

Always, balance and harmony imply careful editing of furnishings and accessories. Sometimes, says designer De Bare Saunders, being out of scale is more interesting than being in scale. "Rules are for students," he says. For John Saladino, there is one abiding principle: "Things that go into a room must have respect for one another, even though those objects may be of totally opposite character. People who just jam everything into a beautiful room risk losing its proportions."

COOL AND CLASSIC

I n the manner of his mentor, master decorator Billy Baldwin, Frank Babb Randolph often works with traditional elements ~ French furniture, fine antiques ~ and his approach often incorporates Baldwin principles such as using inexpensive fabrics on costly pieces of furniture. But the crisp lines of the bedrooms in his own home reveal the soul of a modernist.

Equilibrium in his Washington, D.C., bedroom begins with the bed itself: Centered in the room, it seems to float from the ceiling with the grace of a trapeze. The simple canopy, made from lengths of white cotton suspended from a thin wood frame, is open and airy, yet offers a sense of cozy enclosure. Although the room has 8-foot ceilings, "you feel you've entered a very grand room at least 10 feet tall," says Randolph.

The guest bedroom is as refined and carefully edited as the master bedroom ~ a kind of cool, clean extension of it, with snowy walls and tab curtains of the same burlap-textured linen. In both rooms, found objects such as shells picked up on the beach are mixed with expensive antique furnishings in yet another striking juxtaposition. "These are the things we see in nature," says the designer. "Why shouldn't we live with them?"

In each room, furniture stands out in silhouette against the white walls and woodwork. A quiet backdrop, says Randolph, "makes furniture legs seem to dance."

In the master bedroom (opposite), light floods in through new clean-lined French doors hung with tab curtains of hand-woven Nantucket linen. A fine eighteenth-century chair wears natural-colored woven linen (above); designer Frank Babb Randolph's childhood teddy bear keeps things from becoming too serious.

The designer's democratic approach to decorating is evident in almost every corner, where fine antiques mingle with humbler pieces. In the guest room (above), where a large abstract painting sets the stage for a harmonious scheme of neutrals, an inexpensive wicker trunk for storing extra blankets hobnobs with a serious French antique chair.

Propped on the room's eighteenth-century Italian writing table is a gouache by American artist Willan de Looper (opposite).

*Gomez furnished her
daughter's bedroom with
a nineteenth-century
embossed brass bed
bought in Peru (above
and right). A raspberry-
red-upholstered chair
and red wool paisley bed
throw boldly offset
the predominantly white
color scheme. Light
reflected off the mirror
at the foot of the bed
and through the diaph-
anous bed hangings
imparts a feminine,
ethereal quality.*

Personal Taste

y their very private nature, bedrooms offer an opportunity to express personal style to its utmost. They are the perfect setting for a display of unabashed sentiment or idiosyncratic whimsy. All of us experience a sense of extra freedom and pleasure in decorating the bedroom. Less restricted by practicality than other rooms (the kitchen, certainly, or rooms where the television or computer dominates), we are obliged only to our own taste and comfort.

Comfort is key in the bedroom, and that comfort has a psychological dimension as well as a physical one. The bedroom is a place where our interior universe ~ the worlds of memory and fantasy ~ can come into play in subtle and mysterious ways. In the bedroom, favorite pictures, books, heirlooms, and items of sentimental significance contribute to comfort as much as do soft linens and pillows.

Thankfully, no one look dominates our era, as it did in times past. All the old "rules" have gone by the boards, and here, at the turn of the millennium, there is more room than ever in the bedroom for an individual point of view.

SCENE-STEALING STYLE

A muslin-tented bedroom with a polka-dot floor is not, perhaps, for everyone, but to Maine antiques dealer Corey Daniels, "theatrical" is synonymous with personal style. The room is one of fifteen in Daniels' eighteenth-century farmhouse, all furnished with pieces he had stashed away over the years, never knowing exactly where he would use them. Eventually they all found places in the house, whose decor may change radically from one season to the next.

He gave the freest rein to his creative impulses in this bedroom. "It started out as a joke, really," Daniels says of the exotic but inviting chamber, which recalls a Napoleonic-era campaign officer's tent. "It's more 'me' than any other room in the house." The quasi-military theme began as an effort to temper the raw, exposed beams of the peaked ceiling and to cover, quickly and cheaply, unattractively painted wainscoting on the walls. Daniels' first proposed solution was to cut up an old canvas tent; failing that, he bought 100-yard rolls of muslin (for less than one dollar a yard) and began draping. The repeating border of heraldic trim that rings the room at the ceiling was cut from corrugated cardboard; it was born as a tongue-in-cheek allusion to tent flaps, as well as an attempt to cover the drapery tacks that held the muslin in place. As an impulsive final touch, Daniels decided to introduce pattern on the putty-colored wood floor by painting a loose design of white polka-dots.

A definitively masculine atmosphere prevails from the furniture to the accents: a brass campaign bed of the mid-nineteenth century, a heavy vintage trunk at its foot, the weighty terra-cotta jars from Crete, and an American pier table, all part of a subtle, muted palette of browns and golds.

A brass campaign bed, a sturdy spool-turned Victorian armchair, and an Anglo-Indian ebony chair emphasize the very masculine mood of Corey Daniels' tentlike bedroom. An American marble-topped pier table with columns serves as a miniature stage for an ever-changing array of objects, at present a vase with a painted profile and a serious-looking set of leather-bound books.

A pair of crossed spears
and a costume jacket
from a Shakespearean
play hanging against
the muslin drapery form
a studied still life (left).
The pieces make wry
reference to theater and
military campaigns,
both of which inspired
the room's decor. Gigantic
terra-cotta jars occupy
an unlikely perch near
the ceiling.

In contrast with
the meticulously staged
master bedroom, the guest
bedroom (opposite) has
a more tranquil and
generic ambience. Anybody
can be comfortable in this
nearly all-white room.

LAYERS OF MEANING

A bed angled rakishly in the bay window and taffeta curtains of pinkest pink are the first clues that here is a very nonconforming stylist indeed. Collage artist and textile designer Carolyn Quartermaine, who also owns a fabric and furnishings shop on London's fashionable Sloane Street, combines the avant-garde artist's sensibility with the traditionalist's predilection for pedigreed antique furnishings. "My style is a blend of the baroque and the contemporary," says Quartermaine. "I take things from the past and use fabrics and color to bring them up to date."

She approaches decorating the same way. "My environments have a sense of collage, of a buildup of paper, fabric, and furniture," she says. "I love hidden layers, revealed one at a time." In her delightfully glamorous London apartment-cum-workshop, part eighteenth-century French chateau and part present-day atelier, Quartermaine offers a decidedly contemporary take on the so-called feminine bedroom. Her own signature silks dress late-nineteenth-century Italian chairs; scribbled over with antique calligraphy, the fabrics take their inspiration from old French script and Mozart manuscripts. Eclectic flea-market finds and humble objects hobnob with formal antique furniture, which is angled casually against white walls with a modernist spareness that is clearly of this century.

Carolyn Quartermaine's roomful of unabashedly original flourishes includes the artist's hand-painted fabrics on a bench and gilded antique chairs, and a shock of brightest pink taffeta at the window. The nineteenth-century French bed "floats" away from the window into the center of the room.

Constantly changing
tableaux grace every
horizontal surface in
Quartermaine's
bedroom. On a marble
mantel (above left),
five carefully positioned
pinecones share space
with old glass vases
and a powder dish, as
well as with one of
Quartermaine's collages.

A lucite hat stand and
other personal treasures
make up a second
vignette (above right).
Mozart's manuscripts
inspired the artwork.
Stretched across a
bench is another of
Quartermaine's hand-
painted silks ~ this
one featuring cut-out
birdlike forms.

A *flotilla of late-nineteenth-century gilded Italian chairs wears Quartermaine's calligraphy-inspired silks. "I like the look of calligraphy, not what it says," the designer explains. "When I make collages out of calligraphy scraps, they take on a language of their own." The "door" between bedroom and bath is a simple, unadorned curtain; a peek into the romantic marble bathroom reveals a plaster copy of a Roman woman's head.*

CUTTING-EDGE CRAFTS

Stepping into the Manhattan apartment of Susie Elson, former chairwoman of the American Crafts Council and long-time crafts collector, is like entering a mad, mad world where the very idea of furniture has been wittily, sometimes bizarrely, reinvented. "It's far out of the ordinary," acknowledges Elson, who shares her high-ceilinged duplex with her husband, Edward Elliott Elson, the United States ambassador to Denmark. To achieve this pointedly individualistic decor, Elson commissioned all the furnishings from top artisans in their field.

Like a modern-day Medici, Elson is a patron of the art furniture world, giving craftspeople the freedom to create one-of-a-kind designs. "These are the antiques of the future," she believes. Things made years ago under her farsighted patronage still look very much of the moment. "If something is genuinely exciting," she says, "it

will continue to be so." As if to prove the point, all the rooms in the sunlit apartment are filled with wonderful handcrafted oddities ~ including a cubist-inspired grand piano with exaggerated geometric planes and trapezoidal legs and twisted-metal chairs in the shape of human figures. "I like things that have a sense of humor, that are on the cutting edge," she says.

In the master bedroom, the dominating presence is a contemporary interpretation of a historic four-poster bed, the posts punched through with Swiss-cheese-like holes. The guest bedroom, in turn, features a writing table and chair from an avant-garde Japanese workshop; its adjoining sitting room nods to craftsmen of the past with a showcase filled with Greek and Roman antiquities. "A bedroom is a place where one spends a great deal of time," says Elson. "It should have joie de vivre, not be staid or humdrum."

In the guest bedroom, a freewheeling mix of animal-print fabrics dresses the bed. In one corner a Japanese writing table holds a collection of ceramic bowls and framed prints; the chair, also Japanese, is distinguished by a metal sunburst back and a seat of lacquered wood. The sitting room beyond is furnished with a classic piece by Le Corbusier and a postmodern tower cabinet from Germany.

61

For the master bedroom
(right), Edward Zucca
made a four-poster
bed of bleached maple,
then finished it with silver
leaf and black ebony
detailing. A glass-top
table by Peter Pierborn
has seven unmatching
ebony legs (above).
The aluminum wing-back
angel chair, by Mark
Brazier-Jones, features
a plump upholstered
velvet seat sitting atop
legs with eyeballs.

Surface Appearances

t all begins with the envelope ~ floors, ceilings, walls, and even windows. The surfaces that enclose a bedroom ~ whether a snug guest hideaway tucked under a sloping roof or a sleek and spacious master suite ~ define its proportions and give the space its basic character. From these fundamental relationships a design can evolve. Sometimes one compelling physical attribute can be the starting point for the design that follows. Perhaps the ceilings are rustic wood beams of an old country church, or the walls are made of translucent glass block, or there is an expanse of beautifully aged wood floors.

Often the dictates of location or even climate are so important that choices of materials are narrowed down. Tile makes more sense than carpet in an Arizona bedroom, for example, while windows with a magnificent view require a different approach from those that face a busy street.

Even if the starting point is an unadorned room with walls of simple sheetrock and floors of plain wood, it is an invitation to the designer to address the envelope ~ and perhaps even push it a bit.

To sound an upbeat
note in this spacious bedroom, designer Gary
Paul chose an unusual,
hand-painted wallpaper
~ a lighthearted takeoff
on a conventional
buttoned-down stripe.
The curtain panels
are made of raw silk. A
new Chinese needlepoint
rug in the Aubusson style
was chosen for the way
its beige ground and mint
green and pink detail tie
in with the wallpaper's
coloring, and for the way
its formal pattern plays
against the verticality of
the painterly walls.

A tiny bedroom
tucked under a steep-
pitched roof in this
Colorado house features
rough plaster and old
wooden beams salvaged
from a tumbledown
building nearby. The
room's enormous
character belies the fact
that this is a newly
built retreat. Lacy bed-
clothes provide an
unexpected counterpoint
to all the rusticity.

The restored flower beds outside ~ originally planted by Louise Beebe Wilder, a famous garden writer of the early 1900s ~ inspired the decor of this country bedroom in upstate New York. Designer David Easton installed new French doors so that the room would "reach out to nature." Oak ceiling beams stained to look old remind the owner of summers spent in France. The French terra-cotta tile floor "flows" in from adjoining rooms.

"Bringing the outside in" was a tenet of mid-century modernism; this house, designed by Bauhaus architect Marcel Breuer in the 1950s, is almost an extension of the natural landscape. In one bedroom (opposite), *walls of rugged Maryland stone, carefully placed to show off its shape and color, create a powerful abstract composition. The huge glass sliding doors extend the space visually into the woods. In another bedroom (above), a* *bluestone floor is a cool complement to the woven grasscloth "wainscoting" and nubby wall hangings. The wall-hung desk and credenza echo the low horizontal lines of the house.*

CONCRETE REFLECTIONS

Sunlight, and its reflection on water, are prime elements in the decoration of this contemporary Florida home. All the main rooms in the vast, E-shaped house are organized around a 47-foot swimming pool that comes almost to the ground-level windows. Light bounces off the swimming pool through the square-mullioned, floor-to-ceiling windows, penetrating the house even in winter when the sun is at a low angle. It flickers on white walls and floors made of summerstone, a precast concrete paving material that runs through the house and outside into the pool courtyard. "Water is a great architectural tool," says Washington, D.C., architect Hugh Newell Jacobsen. "It was an intentional part of the design."

In a highly practical choice of materials, the designer paved the master bedroom with the same summerstone, a textured snow-white material that has imprints of coral in it. He continued the summerstone right through the bedroom's sybaritic bath, a freestanding little pavilion linked to the bedroom by a corridor. Nonslippery and treated with waterproof sealant, this flooring is ideal for a house where trekking between the pool and the interior goes on all day. It also helps keep the rooms cool. To minimize the need for air-conditioning, every room was designed with two exposures for cross-ventilation and relies on ceiling fans to keep the air moving.

But the main feature of the house remains the light and its reflections. The bedroom walls and ceilings wear a straightforward coat of flat white paint, forming a clean, contemporary canvas on which light and its interplay on water act out their dramatic roles.

Architect Hugh Newell Jacobsen's passion for classical order and symmetry is expressed in the windows in the master bedroom, which run the full 10 feet from floor to ceiling. Jacobsen also designed the four-poster bed, made of steel pipe with faux bronze finish, specifically for the room.

The bath pavilion, with an oval tub sunk into white summerstone flooring, features a ceiling-high door to the garden beyond (left). A grove of grapefruit trees shields the room from view, but tall louvered shutters can be closed for greater privacy.

The adjoining master bedroom (opposite), a classic white box with unadorned plasterboard walls and ceiling and the same summerstone flooring, might seem antiseptic in cooler climes; in subtropical Florida, its coolness is welcome.

CHAPTER 5

Beds and Beyond

aybed, sleigh bed, or canopy bed ~ a bed is, of course, the one given in a bedroom, and by virtue of its significance as much as its size, it generally occupies center stage. But even given its preeminence, a bed may be imposing or retiring, formal or informal. The traditional four-poster, for example, will immediately assert its sturdy presence in the largest room. But the curtains and lines of the contemporary four-poster can impart a lightness unknown to its medieval forebears.

A simple bed, such as a futon on a platform, will allow other pieces to establish the mood of the room ~ an antique armoire, perhaps, or an inviting armchair. Auxiliary pieces ~ desk, chairs, vanity, nightstand ~ should do more than look pretty. "Everything must be functional," says designer De Bare Saunders. "Even an antique desk should have a useful writing surface, not just be there for decoration."

Freed from the "matched suites" that once enjoyed great popularity, we can forage through history for inspiration. It is only fitting that in this most personal room, furniture is mixed and matched ~ old with new, antiques with reproductions ~ to personalize the space.

Manhattan designer Debra Blair chose reproduction furniture with an exotic Anglo-Indian look ~ a metal bed with a tent-shaped top, left bare except for sheer batiste drapery panels, and a cane and teak "planter's chaise" ~ for a show-house bedroom. Indian rugs over textured sisal on the floor, glazed pomegranate-red walls, and a cerulean-blue ceiling form a rich tableau.

Quirky and colorful, with red and white floral-papered walls and turquoise floors, this bedroom by Brian Murphy of the venerable Parish-Hadley decorating firm is anchored by a four-poster bed with *pineapple finials. An African-American snake quilt (intended to keep evil spirits away while its owner sleeps) and a 1950s circular hooked rug with a sea-creature motif add even more layers of pattern.*

The elegant curvature
of the iron four-poster
bed echoes this bedroom's
distinctive tentlike ceiling.
Atlanta designer Nancy
Braithwaite chose
reproduction pieces for
this house ~ Regency-style
carved gilt armchairs
and a French Empire-
style cherry center table ~
as counterpoints to the
room's contemporary
architecture. Sunny yellow-
striped walls, sumptuous
bed hangings, and white
silk upholstery on the
sofa convey cheerfulness
and elegance in equal
measure. A yellow and
white linen print borders
the white damask bed
hangings, pillows, and
bedskirt, as well as the
Roman shades.

This inviting nap spot
and sometime guest room
occupies one end of a
long narrow kitchen in
the Kansas City house of
decorative arts dealers
Bruce Burstert and
Robert Raymond Smith.
They sought out indige-
nous American furniture
~ a Missouri-made wal-
nut daybed more than
150 years old, a slip-
covered chaise, an
American Queen Anne–
style tea table, and a New
England cupboard
still wearing its original
red paint ~ to comple-
ment the house's colonial
design roots.

Pride of place in this cozy bedroom under the eaves of a Martha's Vineyard seaside estate goes to a custom-made copy of a traditional Empire sleigh bed. The commodious curves of its headboard and footboard make it a compelling focal point in the small room.

For decoration, New York design team Tom Fox and Joe Nahem capitalized on the owners' collection of antique fishing lures. A vintage electric fan hums with a nostalgic whirr.

A *quick and clever
solution to the question
of privacy in a guest
room shared by twin beds
is this freestanding, three-
part screen. Painted
to look like button-tufted
upholstery, the screen
separates the beds, at the
same time effectively
carving out a nook for a
dressing table. Simple
wood bedsteads and
a color scheme of pale
blues and creams create
the feeling of a classic
Swedish country interior.*

Designer Glenn Gissler turned a cozy seaside bedroom into a sitting room with an upholstered twin-size bed (above). A custom-built oak frame and piles of pillows further disguise the bed. An Asian storage box cov-ered with parchment serves as a coffee table.

A charmingly sedate guest bedroom in a rural New Jersey farmhouse is furnished with a French Empire enameled metal sleigh bed and an antique English sewing table used as a night-stand (opposite). The idea, says Jorge Letelier, the architect who owns this weekend home, was to evoke the feeling of a fine old country house in Brittany.

Headboards can be a
functional backrest
and a decorative focal
point of almost architec-
tural importance.
Here, Mariette Himes
Gomez joined twin-
size mahogany Empire
headboards with
bronze d'oré trim to
make a king-size
bed. A tall nineteenth-
century screen behind
the headboard gives the
bed still greater height.

A lacy scrollwork head-
board is the outstanding
decorative feature in
a bedroom where under-
statement rules. Like a
pen and ink drawing on
a blank page, its silhouette
is sharp against the
room's subtle patterns
and textures. On the bed,
for example, though
everything is white, the
matte linen duvet, shams,
and bedskirt contrast
with the sheen of the
pillowcases and top sheet.
A classical medallion
and swag cotton print on
an antique chair at the
foot of the bed is another
decorative flourish.

A fabulous Art Nouveau bentwood bed by the Thonet Brothers furniture makers, found in a Paris flea market, is part of a wide-ranging selection of decorative arts in a Connecticut collector's home (above). The curvaceous loveseat is also a nineteenth-century European bentwood piece. White walls and simple bed dressings allow the strong, sinuous lines to dominate the room.

A distinguished guest bedroom in Jorge Letelier's New Jersey country house features an antique metal bed from Italy, an Empire chair, and a Greek revival urn lamp on a skirted table (opposite). In such refined surroundings, the choice of art on the wall ~ a contemporary painting of suburban houses and mailboxes in lurid colors ~ comes as a bit of a shock. "I find it fresh, friendly, and amusing," says the designer ~ a reminder "not to take things so seriously."

Trim yet glamorous, this bedroom by Los Angeles designer Michael Berman relies on large-scale pieces for impact (left). A sheet-metal sleigh bed with Art Deco curves combines with an imposing fruit-wood armoire (housing an audio-video system), a spirited pair of roll-arm club chairs in bold black and cream stripe, and an oval ottoman with long cord trimming. Celadon green walls form a soothing backdrop. The designer's X-legged writing table and wool-upholstered chair (above), with its voluptuous form and satin-finish legs, take inspiration from such 1940s masters as Jean-Michel Frank and T. H. Robsjohn-Gibbings.

*Genuine antiques mix
unabashedly with
reproductions against the
wood-paneled wall
of a nineteenth-century
farmhouse bedroom
in upstate New York. The
low poster bed ~ simple,
graceful, and strong of
line ~ is newly made, as
are the slipcovered
club chairs and ottoman.
The circular end table
in the foreground
is a contemporary craft
piece. Everything else ~
the faded Oriental rug,
weighty silver candlestick,
vintage velvet throw
pillows, and toile de Jouy
bed covering ~ has
been mellowed and soft-
ened by time.*

There's nothing more gracious or convenient than a separate room reserved for getting dressed. Mariette Himes Gomez took the space seriously, choosing furniture of consequence, including a gleaming Empire dresser and an English chaise longue with a hinged cushion that opens for storage (opposite). Clear panes of glass in all the doors were replaced with mirrors. Beige basket-weave carpeting sets the room apart from the adjoining master bedroom, which has bare floors.

Storage pieces need not always be used in the room for which they were intended. In the Newport, Rhode Island, summer house bedroom of the late interior designer Robert Hill, an antique French kitchen hutch has been pressed into service as a bookcase (above). Its distressed white finish helps the piece blend easily with the white-stained oak floors and soft gray-beige walls that form the pale envelope of the room.

These compact storage
cupboards were designed
by Milan-based architect
Gae Aulenti for a friend's
seaside retreat (left).
In keeping with a week-
end house whose focus
is the outdoors, most of
the furniture is kept
simple and is built-in.

A freestanding storage
unit (opposite) is the
centerpiece of a commodi-
ous dressing room in
a new suburban house
by architects Shelton,
Mindel. Resembling
a giant jewelry box, it
opens on all four sides,
revealing a dressing
table within.

Atlanta decorator Jane Williamson devised a charming, feminine vanity to just fit in front of a sunny window (opposite). The serpentine front was cut from plywood, then smocked like a little girl's dress with red and white ribbon-patterned fabric.

Long Island designer Pat Sayers chose historic lilac-pattern fabric, topped with a piece of lace cutwork, to form the dressing table skirt (right). Beneath the surface is a simple, white-painted plywood box with cubby holes for storage.

SOLID COMFORTS

There is not a piece of furniture in this urbane bedroom designed for a gentleman that does not have serious presence. Each carefully chosen item stands by itself; some, like a Biedermeier bed and turn-of-the-century Austrian desk, are practically small buildings in their own right.

All of this is, of course, no accident. "The room itself was modern and somewhat lackluster," says designer De Bare Saunders, "so we chose furniture of great architectural interest." The pieces were selected individually, not all purchased at one time. "We put little in, but each piece is in scale with the others and with the architecture of the room," says Saunders. The pediment-topped headboard on that remarkable bed, for example, reminds the designer and his partner, Ronald Mayne, of the Italian Renaissance architect Palladio (in the oval is an exquisite oil painting of Mercury tying his shoe). The substantial armchair is a leather reproduction of a classic Art Deco design. Amid all this solidness of form, the charcoal and ivory zebra-striped rug makes a bold graphic statement of its own, as does the striped wallpaper, whose camel color complements the wood tones of the furniture.

What makes it all work? "Everything's very clean-lined, no matter what period or century," says Saunders. "It was all modern for its day."

There are no "throw-away" pieces in this masculine bedroom created by Ronald Mayne and De Bare Saunders. Everything from the austerely simple Austrian desk to the leather armchair stands on solid, almost sculptural ground.

An 1890s gilded
vanity mirror, set within
a Corinthian temple
frame, echoes the
pedimented headboard it
reflects (left). Its richness
is balanced by a tailored
striped chintz on the gentleman's dressing table
and tempered by personal
mementos tucked into
the frame of the mirror.
Painted gold flowers
adorn the backrest of a
Chinese black lacquer
chair. The streamlined
leather armchair offers
an irresistible place
to read (opposite). At the
window, a valance and
cafe curtain of seersucker
trimmed with unfussy
cotton fringe and hung
loosely from curtain
tiebacks allow a soft light
to penetrate the room.

Dressing the Room

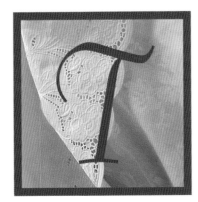

The lavish use of fabric in a bedroom still signifies what it did in Louis XIV's France: luxury. The swags, festoons, and tassels of brocade, damask, and silk in a fashionable seventeenth-century boudoir also provided privacy and a certain degree of warmth against the elements. But by the late nineteenth century, interest in the healthful effects of fresh air led to a much lighter, fresher look. Today, anything goes.

Today's fabrics of choice may be gauzy white cottons, ever-popular chintzes (whose lush floral patterns are still based on nineteenth-century favorites), natty stripes, carefree checks, or restful solids, which can be an antidote to the profusion of pattern often found elsewhere in the house.

Fabric-covered furniture ~ headboard, chairs, skirted vanity ~ provide additional opportunities to experiment. Pretty pleats and even contrasting piping can unify several different pieces and lend a layer of eye-catching detail. In recent years, sheets ~ prehemmed, seamless, and in marvelous patterns ~ have made department stores a wonderful resource for decorating the bedroom.

Oceans of fabric in the colors of sunshine and ripe fruit ~ mainly a printed French cotton combining floral and paisley motifs ~ elevate this grandly proportioned showhouse bedroom to levels of fantasy reminiscent of England's Royal Pavilion in Brighton. The custom canopy, made of thick swags of fabric cascading from a conical crown known as a lit à la Polonaise, and a V-shaped window valance trimmed with tinkly gold bells are delightfully fanciful. "I didn't want anything stodgy or uptight," says designer Barbara Ostrom. Upholstered panels on the headboard and footboard match the fabric on the bolster and bedcover, to add an aura of coziness.

In a room that is a model of Zen understatement, with a controlled palette of sandy neutrals, carefully tailored bed-linens take center stage (above). The soft-toned duvet cover and pillowcases on the low platform bed give the room a contemporary, tailored look. Striped edging and buttons on the pillows are handsome details (left).

Demure, fresh fabrics ~ lacy Victorian whites on the bed, a striped ticking slipcover on a chaise ~ stir memories of childhood summers in the master bedroom of a new Ozark retreat (opposite). The nostalgic atmosphere warms up a sparsely furnished room, whose few pieces are contributions from the owners' relatives and friends.

There is no shortage of fabric in this serene creation by Boston designer Benn Theodore (opposite). A cushioned upholstered headboard in cream cotton harmonizes with the clipped Swiss batiste bed hangings that dress the four-poster. European linens cover a profusion of pillows.

A matching bench curls up at the foot of the bed.

A Connecticut antiques dealer who loves the plain lines of Shaker furniture created these tidy-as-a-bandbox bed enclosures (above). Fresh and crisp, the draped alcoves provide drama in a Shaker-plain guest room.

The headboards, bed-skirts, and canopy linings of blue plaid are in simple but striking contrast to the expanses of white.

Fabric gives the interior of this Derbyshire gatehouse in England its cheerful demeanor. Sunny yellow enlivens the polka-dot walls and the exuberant floral chintz curtains. A delicate red and white stripe covers the whimsically shaped headboard, while broader and bolder versions of the stripe appear on the bedspread and pillow.

In a small London bed-
room, decorator Lady
Jane Churchill took a cue
from France, where bed-
rooms are often decorated
with just one patterned
fabric. Here a charming
red and white toile de
Jouy upholsters the walls
and headboard and
swaths the windows. A
rosy red braided trim is
used to highlight curtain
details and give the
scheme greater definition.
White lace-trimmed
linens and pillows make
the bed an oasis of calm.

TAILOR-MADE TRANQUILITY

Soothing is the word for this bedroom by designers Charles Spada and Tom Vanderbeck. The color gray, which is often underrated and surprisingly versatile, is the key to this pleasant effect. "I love gray in bedrooms because it's soft, ethereal, and calming," says Spada.

To make the room look all of a piece despite its collection of antique furnishings from disparate sources, the designers used a palette of grays and limited the number of fabrics to just a few unfussy ones. "Forget about heavy lace, chintzes, and brocades," says Spada. "Keep a bedroom minimal, so it's not overbearing. In a bedroom you want to feel calm, not be distracted by a mishmash of things."

For the curtains, tailored bedskirt, headboard, and chaise longue, Spada and Vanderbeck chose a cotton-linen blend, a material they find more practical than linen, which tends to rumple. The custom-made draperies feature inverted pleats, rather than the more traditional pinch pleats, to achieve a richer, fuller, more refined look. A pair of late-nineteenth-century painted French chairs are covered in linen; a little gold footstool is upholstered in gray silk taffeta. Touches of white ~ a strip of edging along the bottom of the bedskirt, simple bed linens ~ provide a refreshing contrast.

Not a ruche or a ruffle finds its way into this smart, tailored bedroom. The headboard is upholstered in a soft gray cotton-linen blend; the bedskirt is of the same fabric edged in white. "Bedrooms shouldn't be overfrilly and suffocating," believes designer Charles Spada. "You can come into this room, take a deep breath, and forget the world."

Consistency of color in fabric and paint unifies an assortment of antique European pieces (left). An eighteenth-century French chaise, still bearing its original paint, and the headboard (above) have been upholstered in a durable cotton-linen blend. The demilune commode has a coat of distressed paint that matches the gray fabric.

CHAPTER 7

Final Touches

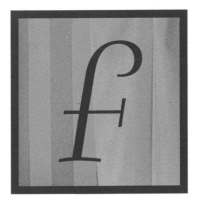

or many of us when it comes to accessorizing a bedroom, minimalism is not a very appealing concept. Sentimental souvennirs should find a natural home here ~ a pair of antique candlesticks, a vintage radio, some seashells from a vacation, beloved family photographs, favorite books. Together they contribute to the sense of well-being that is the essence of every successful bedroom.

Unlike large pieces of furniture, accents ~ small collectibles, pillows, artwork, for example ~ are easy to vary. Since we spend a lot of time in the bedroom it is important to head off visual ennui. One antiques dealer suggests removing all small objects from time to time and creating new vignettes by bringing pieces out of storage or borrowing them from other rooms. Careful placement and well-conceived displays can make even the most ordinary accessories seem special. "Every object needs a home," says New York designer Mariette Himes Gomez. "When your possessions don't have a home in your bedroom, they're simply clutter. When they're well organized, they become collections."

The repetition of a
single simple shape pro-
duces a striking wall
display in this bedroom
by decorator Jeff Lincoln.
With little else to distract
the eye, the two tiers
of six framed antique
engravings, viewed
through the lines of an
undraped iron four-
poster, create a harmo-
nious geometry. A pair of
white plaster table
lamps on either side of
the bed, reproductions of
a classic Giacometti
disc design of the 1940s,
underscores the room's
decisive symmetry.
A carved wooden pineap-
ple, once a finial on
the roof of an old build-
ing, was chosen for
its sculptural quality
and hefty scale.

Sparkling accessories play off an intense backdrop of sage-green walls in a crisply elegant bedroom by designers Lee Bierly and Christopher Drake (left). Against this color a gilt-framed bull's-eye mirror stands out. Beneath, an antique mirrored chest is home to a framed drawing on an easel and a pair of candlestick lamps.

Glints of gold and hints of grandeur reminiscent of the Old South are artfully combined in a Louisiana bedroom by designers Ann Holden and Ann Dupuy (opposite). The gold beaded lampshade and gilt sunburst mirror frames add iridescent detail. The cherub hanging from the wrought-iron bed frame adds an unexpected note of whimsy.

A purist ethic, very much in keeping with the traditional Japanese approach to choosing and positioning objects, is at work in this Manhattan high-rise bedroom belonging to design consultant Robert Homma. A century-old statue of Buddha sits atop a lacquered table (opposite). The screen, a contemporary piece made of handmade paper, was picked up at a department store sale. A trio of boldly patterned shells creates a strong still life on a patterned bench. Green vases by a Japanese ceramicist are arrayed on a nineteenth-century scholar's bench traditionally used for calligraphy (above). A contemporary red and gold Japanese lacquer box is used for photo storage, while Shunga prints and woodcuts are propped casually against the wall.

Even books become decorative accessories when displayed in a glass-fronted Empire bookcase with old-world charm (opposite). The all-white pottery on the cabinet is one of several collections grouped by color in the Victorian farmhouse of designer Jorge Letelier.

An ever-changing array of objects and art-work marks the decorating style of antiques dealer Corey Daniels (right). This studied bedside arrangement is composed of vintage treasures: twin mercury glass vases, old framed photographs, and an alabaster decanter.

HOMESPUN TRADITION

A love for all things old and handcrafted informs the decor of two bedrooms in the studio of Bob Timberlake, a painter of the American Realist school who also is something of a cultural historian. Timberlake oversees the production of a line of furniture and accessories that captures and preserves the Arts and Crafts heritage of North Carolina, his home state.

To complement native folk furnishings found in the area ~ pie safes with hand-punched tin panels, painted chests, and twig rockers, for example ~ Timberlake collects and reproduces homespun accessories. Among them are quilts, coverlets, pottery (including agateware pitchers), birdhouses, and decoys. All are locally made in the manner of master craftspeople of the past. Pottery bowls are hand thrown and decorated with simple red, blue, and brown glazes typical of the region. Rag rugs are woven on looms just as they were a century ago. Wooden furniture such as beds and chairs are finished to show off the distinctive grains of native cherry and walnut.

Above all, Timberlake appreciates "the way things were made with such love and affection back in the old days," with an innate love of materials ~ the woods, the homespun, the clay ~ that were transformed into furniture, quilts, and pots to be cherished.

The rough-hewn beams and small window of a restored 1807 log home form an authentic setting for reproduction furnishings and accessories with roots in rural North Carolina crafts traditions. In the master bedroom, a chest is hand-painted with Pennsylvania Dutch motifs, and a new quilt reproduces the vivid log cabin pattern. A collection of beautifully framed silhouettes punctuates the geometry of the log-chinking walls.

Vintage toys recalling
a country childhood ~
birchbark canoes on
the wall, a red metal truck
on a sidetable ~ acces-
sorize a guest bedroom in
Bob Timberlake's studio.
A wall shelf above the easy
chair holds a handful
of miniatures. A rag rug,
camp blankets, and boldly
striped bed covers bring
high color to the rustic
decor. Worn blue paint on
a reproduction cabinet
convincingly simulates age.

Directory of Designers and Architects

Gae Aulenti
Dott.Arch.Gae.Aulenti
Milan, Italy

Michael Berman
Michael Berman Design
Los Angeles, California

Lee Bierly
Bierly-Drake
Boston, Massachusetts

Debra Blair
Blair Design Associates, Inc.
New York, New York

Nancy Braithwaite
Nancy Braithwaite Interiors, Inc.
Atlanta, Georgia

Bruce Burstert
Robert Raymond Smith Oriental
    Rugs and Bruce Burstert
    Decorative Arts
Kansas City, Missouri

Manuel Canovas
Manuel Canovas, Inc.
New York, New York

Paul Canvasser
PDC Designer
Birmingham, Michigan

Jane Churchill
Jane Churchill Interiors Ltd.
London, England

Celeste Cooper
Repertoire
Boston, Massachusetts

Corey Daniels
Corey Daniels Antiques
Wells, Maine

Christopher Drake
Bierly-Drake
Boston, Massachusetts

Ann Dupuy
Holden & Dupuy
New Orleans, Louisiana

David Easton
David Anthony Easton, Inc.
New York, New York

Mark Epstein
Mark Epstein Associates
New York, New York

Richard Eustice
Atlantic House Ltd.
Boston, Massachusetts

Tom Fox
Fox-Nahem Design
New York, New York

Lynn Gerhard
Gerhard Designs
Islip, New York

Glenn Gissler
Glenn Gissler Design, Inc.
New York, New York

Mariette Himes Gomez
Gomez Associates
New York, New York

Carolyn Guttilla
Carolyn Guttilla / Plaza One
Locust Valley, New York

Albert Hadley
Parish-Hadley Associates
New York, New York

Ann Holden
Holden & Dupuy
New Orleans, Louisiana

Cathi and Steven House
House + House
San Francisco, California

Hugh Newell Jacobsen
Hugh Newell Jacobsen
Washington, D.C.

Jorge Letelier
Letelier-Rock Design, Inc.
New York, New York

Jeffrey T. Lincoln
Jeffrey Lincoln Interiors Inc.
Locust Valley, New York

Ronald Mayne
Stingray Hornsby Antiques
    and Interiors
Watertown, Connecticut

Lee Mindel
Shelton, Mindel and Associates
New York, New York

Brian Murphy
Parish-Hadley Associates, Inc.
New York, New York

Joe Nahem
Fox-Nahem Design
New York, New York

Barbara Ostrom
Barbara Ostrom Associates, Inc.
Mahwah, New Jersey

Gary Paul
Gary Paul Design, Inc.
New York, New York

Peter Pennoyer
Peter Pennoyer Architects PC
New York, New York

Carolyn Quartermaine
London, England

Frank Babb Randolph
Frank Babb Randolph Interior
    Design
Washington, D.C.

Craig Raywood
Craig Raywood Design, 401 Ltd.
New York, New York

Katie Ridder
Peter Pennoyer Architects PC
New York, New York

Spruce Roden
VSF
New York, New York

John Saladino
John F. Saladino, Inc.
New York, New York

De Bare Saunders
Stingray Hornsby Antiques
    and Interiors
Watertown, Connecticut

Pat Sayers
Design Resources of Long
    Island Inc.
Huntington, New York

Peter Shelton
Shelton, Mindel and Associates
New York, New York

Robert Raymond Smith
Robert Raymond Smith Oriental
    Rugs and Bruce Burstert
    Decorative Arts
Kansas City, Missouri

Charles Spada
Charles Spada Interiors
Boston, Massachusetts

Alexandra Stoddard
Alexandra Stoddard, Inc.
New York, New York

Yves Taralon
Yves-Germain Taralon
    Decoration
Richebourg, France

Benn Theodore
Benn Theodore, Inc.
Boston, Massachusetts

Tom Vanderbeck
T. F. Vanderbeck Antiques
    and Interiors
Hadlyme, Connecticut

Peter Wheeler
P. J. Wheeler Associates
Boston, Massachusetts

Jane Williamson
Jane Williamson Antiques
    and Design
Atlanta, Georgia

The room on page 1 was designed by Jane Churchill; page 2, Vincent Dané; page 7, Barbara Deichman; page 8, Bruce Burstert and Robert Raymond Smith; page 11, Ann Holden and Ann Dupuy; page 16, Lynn Gerhard; page 34, Celeste Cooper; page 50, Craig Raywood; page 64, Cathi and Steven House; page 76, Nancy Braithwaite; page 126, Charles Spada; page 142, Robert Hill.

Photography Credits

1	Christopher Simon Sykes	66	James Yochum	109	Kari Haavisto
2	Michael Dunne	67	Laurie E. Dickson	110-111	Jeff McNamara
4	Kari Haavisto	68-69	John Vaughan	112	Esto/Scott Frances (top and bottom)
7	J. Merrell	70-71	Walter Smalling	113	Richard Felber
8	Peter Margonelli	72	Robert Lautman	114	Eric Roth
11	Lizzie Himmel	74-75	Robert Lautman	115	David Phelps
12	Kari Haavisto	76	Jack Winston	116	Jacques Dirand
15	Scott Frances	78	Jeff McNamara	117	Walter Smalling
16	Jeff McNamara	79	Jeff McNamara	118-119	Jeff McNamara
18	Richard Felber	80-81	Langdon Clay	120	Simon Wheeler
20-21	Richard Felber	82	Peter Margonelli	121	Christopher Simon Sykes
22	Antoine Bootz	83	Lizzie Himmel	122	Jeff McNamara
24-25	Antoine Bootz	84-85	Scott Frances	124-125	Jeff McNamara
26	Lizzie Himmel	86	Andrew Bordwin	126	Antoine Bootz
28-29	Lizzie Himmel	87	Jeff McNamara	128-129	Peter Margonelli
30	Antoine Bootz	88	Antoine Bootz	130	Eric Roth
32-33	Antoine Bootz	89	William Waldron	131	Lizzie Himmel
34	Tom Yee	90	Catherine Leuthold	132-133	Antoine Bootz
36-39	Gordon Beall	91	Jeff McNamara	134	Jeff McNamara
40	Antoine Bootz	92-93	Grey Crawford	135	Thibault Jeanson
42-43	Antoine Bootz	94-95	Kari Haavisto	136	Langdon Clay
44	Thibault Jeanson	96	Antoine Bootz	138-139	Langdon Clay
46-49	Thibault Jeanson	97	Thibault Jeanson	142	Thibault Jeanson
50	Antoine Bootz	98	Antoine Bootz		
52	Thibault Jeanson	99	Langdon Clay		
54-55	Thibault Jeanson	100	Walter Smalling		
56	Jacques Dirand	101	Jeff McNamara		
58-60	Jacques Dirand	102	Kit Latham		
62-63	Jacques Dirand	104-105	Kit Latham		
64	Christopher Irion	106	Kari Haavisto		
		108	Elizabeth Zeschin		

Acknowledgments

House Beautiful would like to thank the following homeowners: Jeffrey and Sharon Casdin, Lynn and Kurt Kircher, Pat Guthman, David and Katrin Cargill, Dolph Leuthold, Suzanne and Elliott West.

The photograph on page 16 was taken at the Mansions and Millionaires Showhouse, Sands Point, New York; page 34, the Boston Design Center, Boston, Massachusetts; page 66, the Park Ridge Youth Campus Showhouse, Wilmette, Illinois; page 78, the Mansions in May Showhouse, Morristown, New Jersey; pages 79 and 86, the Southampton Showhouse, Southampton, New York; page 88, the Royal Oak Foundation Showhouse, New York, New York; pages 92 and 93, the Pasadena Showhouse, Pasadena, California; page 96, the Royal Oak Foundation Showhouse, New York, New York; page 100, the Atlanta Symphony Associates Decorators Showhouse, Atlanta, Georgia; page 101, the Mansions and Millionaires Showhouse, Sands Point, New York; pages 102-105, the Litchfield County Designer Showhouse, Roxbury, Connecticut; pages 110-111, the Mansions in May Showhouse, Morristown, New Jersey; page 117, the French Designers Showhouse, New York, New York; pages 118-119, the Junior League of Boston Decorators' Showhouse, Boston, Massachusetts; pages 122-125, the Junior League of Hartford Showhouse, Hartford, Connecticut; pages 128-29, the Locust Valley Showhouse, Locust Valley, New York; page 130, the Junior League of Boston 25th Anniversary Decorator Show House, Boston, Massachusetts.